WHAT ARE SEA PLANTS AND ALGAE?

LYNNAE D. STEINBERG

Britannica®
Educational Publishing

IN ASSOCIATION WITH

ROSEN
EDUCATIONAL SERVICES

Published in 2017 by Britannica Educational Publishing (a trademark of Encyclopædia Britannica, Inc.) in association with The Rosen Publishing Group, Inc.
29 East 21st Street, New York, NY 10010

Distributed exclusively by Rosen Publishing.
To see additional Britannica Educational Publishing titles, go to rosenpublishing.com.

First Edition

Britannica Educational Publishing
J.E. Luebering: Executive Director, Core Editorial
Mary Rose McCudden: Editor, Britannica Student Encyclopedia

Rosen Publishing
Jacob R. Steinberg: Editor
Nelson Sá: Art Director
Nicole Russo: Designer
Cindy Reiman: Photography Manager
Sherri Jackson: Photo Researcher

Library of Congress Cataloging-in-Publication Data

Names: Steinberg, Lynnae D., 1957–
Title: What are sea plants and algae? / Lynnae D. Steinberg.
Description: New York : Britannica Educational Publishing in association with Rosen Educational Services, 2017. | Series: Let's find out! Marine life | Audience: Grades 1–4. | Includes bibliographical references and index.
Identifiers: LCCN 2016022226 | ISBN 9781508103929 (library bound) | ISBN 9781508103936 (pbk.) | ISBN 9781508103172 (6-pack)
Subjects: LCSH: Marine plants—Juvenile literature. | Algae—Juvenile literature.
Classification: LCC QK103 .S74 2017 | DDC 581.7—dc23
LC record available at https://lccn.loc.gov/2016022226

Manufactured in China

CONTENTS

Sea Plants and Algae

Eelgrass has adapted so that it may live most of its life completely underwater.

Plants grow nearly everywhere on Earth, including in the water. Plants are vital to life on Earth. They provide food for people and animals. They also make the oxygen that other living things breathe. Water plants, or hydrophytes, are plants that have adapted to life in the water. Some water plants live totally submerged, while

others live only partly in water. All water plants share many similarities, so scientists believe that all water plants originally came from land. Still, they have adapted, or changed, to be able to live under water.

Other organisms, called algae, live in water, too. Algae are very important because they make much of Earth's oxygen, which humans and other animals need to breathe. Some algae, such as seaweed, look like plants. However, algae are neither plants nor animals. Instead they belong to a group of living things called protists.

A carpet of green algae covers the rocks of this seashore.

PHOTOSYNTHESIS

All green plants make their own food using the process called photosynthesis. Photosynthesis requires sunlight, water, a gas called carbon dioxide, and a substance in plants called chlorophyll. Photosynthesis is important because it produces oxygen.

Energy from sunlight fuels the process known as photosynthesis.

THINK ABOUT IT

Why is it important that photosynthesis releases oxygen into the atmosphere? Could you live in a world without oxygen?

Humans and other animals need to breathe in oxygen to survive. Some living things other than plants also make their own food through photosynthesis. Photosynthesis actually began with early forms of bacteria and algae.

The process starts when chlorophyll in plants absorbs energy from sunlight. The light energy is used to change

photosynthesis
sunlight
sugars
oxygen
carbon dioxide
water

Photosynthesis uses sunlight, carbon dioxide, and water to create sugars that help plants grow.

Large water lily leaves float on the surface to absorb the sunlight they need.

water and carbon dioxide into oxygen and nutrients called sugars. The plants use some of the sugars to grow and then store the rest. The oxygen is released back into the air or water.

There are some differences between how photosynthesis occurs above water and how it occurs underwater. Instead of getting carbon dioxide from the air that we breathe, as land plants do, both algae and marine plants (plants that live in salt water) pull carbon dioxide directly from their water environment.

Plants are exposed to the same sunlight that we are. However, plants that are submerged under water have a harder time getting the light they need for photosynthesis than plants that live on land. The amount of light that penetrates water depends on water color, water depth, and how turbid the water is. This is why some marine plants have long stems with large leaves that float closer to the surface of the water. There, they can absorb more light.

VOCABULARY

Water that is **turbid** is cloudy or muddy because of floating sediment or dirt in the water.

What Are Plankton and Phytoplankton?

Countless tiny living things float and drift in the world's oceans. These organisms, or living things, are known as plankton. They include plants, animals, and other kinds of organisms. Plankton that is made up of animals or animal-like organisms is called zooplankton. Plankton that is made up of plants or plant-like organisms is called phytoplankton.

These organisms are often no larger than a single cell. For example, a single-celled type of algae, called a diatom,

Zooplankton are usually too small to see easily. Shown is a magnified view of several different zooplankton.

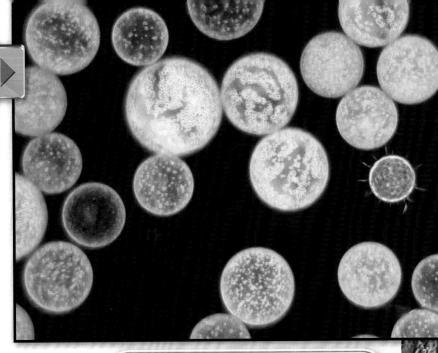

Phytoplankton floats in the water and uses photosynthesis to create energy.

is a common form of phytoplankton. Phytoplankton floats near the surface of the water. Like other plants, phytoplankton undergoes photosynthesis, using sunlight to produce its energy. Besides phytoplankton and zooplankton, bacteria and fungi float in the world's waters. These living things may also be considered plankton.

THINK ABOUT IT

Since most phytoplankton gets its energy through photosynthesis, during which seasons of the year do you think we find larger amounts of phytoplankton in Earth's water?

THE MARINE FOOD CHAIN

The term *food chain* describes the order in which living things depend on each other for food. Every ecosystem has one or more food chains. Most food chains start with organisms that make their own food, such as plants. Scientists call them producers. Organisms that eat other living things are called consumers. Because most living

In an aquatic food web, a predator may eat predators, filterers, and zooplankton.

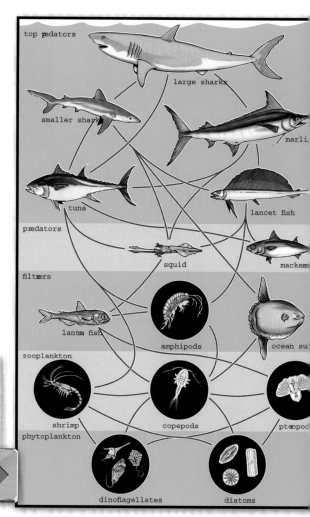

top predators

large sharks

smaller sharks

marli

tuna

lancet fish

predators

squid

macker

filters

lantern fish

amphipods

ocean su

zooplankton

shrimp

copepods

pteopod

phytoplankton

dinoflagellates

diatoms

Tiny phytoplankton, shown here, play a major role in the marine food web.

things eat more than one type of animal or plant, their food chains overlap and connect, creating a food web.

Phytoplankton has an important place in the food chain that supports marine, or sea, animals as well as the humans who eat them. Not only does phytoplankton help produce oxygen, but phytoplankton is also the primary food source, either directly or indirectly, of nearly all sea organisms.

COMPARE AND CONTRAST

Phytoplankton are at the bottom of the marine food chain. Which marine animals do you think are at the top?

ALGAE COME IN MANY COLORS

Algae consist of a large variety of organisms. In general, algae are organisms that are made up of one or more cells that contain chlorophyll. Algae differ from plants in several ways. They do not have stems or leaves, and their roots are different from plant roots. Algae also do not produce flowers or seeds, as plants do. Like plants, however, algae make their own food through photosynthesis.

There are about 27,000 different species, or types, of algae. Many

Chloroplasts are parts of plant and algal cells that contain chlorophyll.

14

types of algae consist of single cells. Other types can form colonies. Algae can be many colors, including red, brown, or green. No matter what their external color, most contain some of the green pigment chlorophyll. Algae vary greatly in size.

COMPARE AND CONTRAST
In what ways are algae and sea plants different? What features do they share in common?

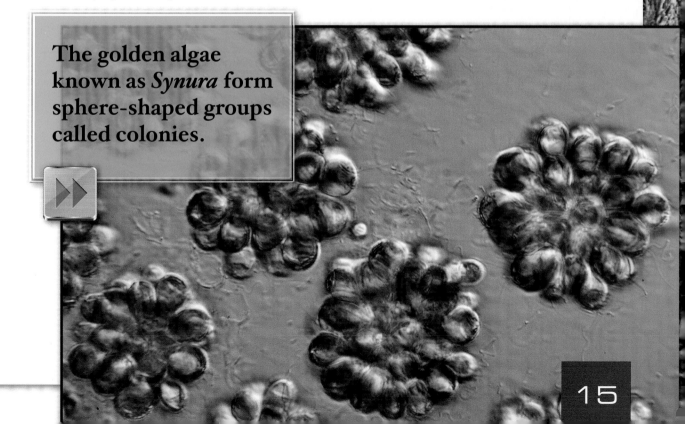

The golden algae known as *Synura* form sphere-shaped groups called colonies.

RED ALGAE

There are more than 5,200 species of red algae. The majority of red algae live in tropical marine habitats, or warm parts of oceans. Most species are multicellular, meaning they have more than one cell. Red algae go through several stages of development to complete their life cycle. The red pigment in red algae allows it to absorb sunlight deep beneath the water's surface.

Many different marine animals feed on this type of red algae known as *Jania rubens*.

A number of species of red algae are harvested for food. These include laver, dulse, and Irish moss. Laver is the source of nori, dried thin sheets of seaweed popular in Japanese cuisine. Irish moss is used in puddings, tooth paste, and ice cream. Some species of red algae are important in forming coral reefs and islands.

Irish moss is a type of red algae used in many of the foods that humans eat.

BROWN ALGAE

Brown algae can be seen along coasts and floating in the ocean. The algae called kelp can reach 200 feet (60 meters) in length. Some can cling to rocks at the bottom of the water using structures called holdfasts. They have stalks (much like plant stems) and wide blades that are similar to leaves. These blades have small pockets of air, called bladders, which aid in lifting them up toward the water's surface.

The air pockets on knotted wrack, a type of brown algae, help it float in the ocean.

A large free-floating mass of brown algae lies in an area of the western Atlantic Ocean known as the Sargasso Sea. This algae, called *Sargassum*, is used by eels, turtles, marlins, sharks, and dolphinfish as a spawning site, or a place to reproduce. Christopher Columbus came upon this patch of algae as he sailed toward the New World. The large mass of algae led him to think that land was near and encouraged him to continue.

THINK ABOUT IT

Why would it be important that brown algae blades float up toward the surface of the water?

Sargassum seaweed forms large masses as it floats along the ocean surface.

Green Algae

Most green algae occur in fresh water. Only about 10 percent of green algae are marine. In the marine environment some are free-floating, but most live on shore rocks. Some species, such as sea lettuce, are eaten by humans. Several species live on land. Some green algae form branched filaments that look like thin wires, hollow balls of cells, or broad, flat sheets.

Green algae are a vital link in the food chain. They are also an important source of oxygen. Nevertheless, they can also be the source of problems. Under certain

Many types of seaweed, like this *Caulerpa prolifera*, are green algae.

conditions, many types of green algae undergo rapid and uncontrolled growth. When this happens, a "bloom" covers the water surface, blocking light from reaching the lower depths. This can have a negative impact on other sea plants and animals.

THINK ABOUT IT

What organisms in ocean environments might be affected by a loss of light?

Some algal blooms not only block sunlight but also become toxic to other marine life.

SEAWEEDS

The large red, brown, and green algae that are found in the oceans are also known as seaweeds. In northern areas, the seaweeds form an almost continuous film over the rocks. In colder Arctic and Antarctic waters they extend to great depths.

In the warm tropics they are found on the floors of lagoons, and they are associated with coral reefs and island atolls. Seaweeds can be bad for coral because they produce harmful chemicals and block the sunlight. However, recent studies have shown that seaweed can protect coral from harmful sea stars.

The seaweeds that wash up on beaches and other shores are actually algae.

Some species are made up of molecules that have the ability to thicken just about any liquid. More than 100,000 metric tons of these molecules are removed from seaweed each year for a variety of uses. Seaweed's ability to filter and clean water makes it useful as a means to extract toxins from wastewater.

Shown is a type of red seaweed. Seaweed can be red, brown, or green algae.

ALONG THE OCEAN'S SHORE

Mangroves are trees or bushes that grow along seashores. They have a thick tangle of roots that stick up through the mud. These roots help to keep waves from washing away the dirt and sand of the coastline. The trees can grow in salty water because they are able to filter out the salt.

Sea grasses have roots and leaves and produce flowers and seeds. They provide valuable habitats to many invertebrates like clams, crabs, and oysters as well as many

As water levels lower, the roots of mangroves become more visible above the water.

Many different sea invertebrates use sea-grass beds as habitats to feed and take shelter.

fish species. Sea-grass beds are the feeding grounds of thousands of different animal species around the world. Sea turtles, manatees, and geese are a few of the animals that eat sea grass. Sea grasses often have fun names such as paddle grass, turtle grass, and manatee grass.

COMPARE AND CONTRAST

Sea grasses and mangroves both grow along the ocean's edge. How are they alike? How are they different?

Is It Too Hot?

The average surface temperature on Earth is slowly increasing. This trend is known as global warming. Warm temperatures are causing the polar ice to melt and ocean waters to rise, changing our shorelines. Increasing water temperature may also cause the growth of harmful algal blooms (HABs). HABs are colonies of algae that grow out of control. These may cause harm to the health of marine life because the

This sign warns visitors about harmful algal blooms in the water.

WARNING

HARMFUL ALGAE MAY BE PRESENT
IN THIS WATER
USE OR CONTACT MAY CAUSE SERIOUS
HARM TO HUMANS AND ANIMALS

FOR FURTHER INFORMATION
CONTACT:

GOULBURN-MURRAY
WATER

GOULBURN-MURRAY
WATER

EMERGENCY   000
Goulburn-Murray Water   1800 064 184

HABs produce toxins. In turn, humans can also be affected by eating fish or other organisms that contain the toxins.

Another effect of HABs is that they may block the amount of light entering the water. This means less photosynthesis occurs and less oxygen enters the oceans. Too little oxygen in the ocean can cause many fish to die.

HABs can reduce the water's oxygen content, poison aquatic animals, and cause breathing and skin problems in humans.

A Spa from the Sea

People visit spas to feel healthy and revitalized. Many sea plants and algae are collected for health and nutritional uses. Some spas use algae therapy to help relax and revitalize their customers. They offer algae or seaweed wraps that they claim soothes the skin and improves circulation. Red algae is a popular food

Nori is a type of seaweed used to make sushi, a popular type of Japanese food.

COMPARE AND CONTRAST

Aquaculture, or ocean farming, is the process of harvesting plants and organisms from the ocean for food. How might this process be different from farming on land?

among vegetarians. Like meat, red algae has a high protein content and high levels of the vitamin B12.

People also eat other types of algae. Ulva, or sea lettuce, is a type of green algae. It is often included in salads and soups. Sea lettuce is rich in iodine and in vitamins A, B, and C. Brown seaweeds are used to make jams, spray whipped cream, pie filling, gravy, and popsicles. You might even find the rich minerals from algae in your medicine or makeup!

Seaweed salads are another form of algae that humans eat.

GLOSSARY

absorb To take in or suck or swallow up.

aquatic Growing or living in or often found in water.

bacteria Any group of single-celled organisms that live in soil, water, or the bodies of plants and animals.

blade The broad flat part of leaves.

cell One of the tiny units that are the basic building blocks of living things.

chlorophyll The green coloring matter of plants that is necessary for photosynthesis.

coast The land near a shore.

colony A population of plants or animals in a particular place that belong to one species.

ecosystem A system made up of an ecological community of living things interacting with their environment especially under natural conditions.

extend To stretch out or reach across a distance.

fungi Living things (like molds and mushrooms) that don't have chlorophyll, live on dead or decaying matter, and were formerly considered plants.

habitat The place or type of place where a plant or animal naturally or normally lives or grows.

harvested To be gathered in a crop.

hydrophyte A plant growing in water or in waterlogged soil.

mass A large amount or number of something.

nutrients Things a plant or animal needs in order to live and grow.

organism A living thing.

protist An organism that resembles plants or animals or both, is one-celled, and that typically includes most algae.

restrict To keep within bounds or limits.

toxin A substance produced by a living organism that is very poisonous to other organisms.

tropical Relating to warm areas of Earth near the Equator.

FOR MORE INFORMATION

Books

Bang, Molly, and Penny Chisholm. *Ocean Sunlight: How Tiny Plants Feed the Sea.* New York, NY: Blue Sky Press, 2012.

Collis, Carolyn. *Seaweed.* Wellington, NZ: Summer Rose Books, 2014.

De la Bedoyere, Camilla. *100 Facts: Plant Life.* Essex, UK: Miles Kelly, 2015.

Hewitt, Sally. *A Walk by the Seaside.* London, UK: Franklin Watts, 2012.

Lawrence, Ellen. *Water Plants: All Wet.* New York, NY: Bearport Publishing, 2016.

Lundgren, Julie K. *Plants Make Their Own Food.* Vero Beach, FL: Rourke Publishing, 2012.

Websites

Because of the changing nature of internet links, Rosen Publishing has developed an online list of websites related to the subject of this book. This site is updated regularly. Please use this link to access this list:

http://www.rosenlinks.com/LFO/seaplant

INDEX